LIBERTY TREE

Tom Paulin

LIBERTY TREE

faber and faber
LONDON·BOSTON

First published in 1983
by Faber and Faber Limited
3 Queen Square London WC1N 3AU
Set by Goodfellow & Egan Limited, Cambridge
Printed in Great Britain by
Whitstable Litho Ltd, Whitstable, Kent

British Library Cataloguing in Publication Data

Paulin, Tom
Liberty tree.
I. Title
821'.914   PR6066.A/
ISBN 0 571 13025 9

For Oswyn, Surinderjit and Jasvinder

Contents

Acknowledgements

Some of these poems have appeared in: *Encounter, Honest Ulsterman, London Review of Books, New Statesman, Poetry Book Society Christmas Supplement, Poetry Review, Quarto,* the *Irish Times, The Times Literary Supplement, The Writers: A Sense of Ireland, Threshold,* and some have also appeared in a pamphlet, *The Book of Juniper.* 'Martello' was written to commemorate the centenary of James Joyce's birth and was originally published in *James Joyce and Modern Literature,* edited by W. J. McCormack and Alistair Stead (Routledge & Kegan Paul, 1982).

I am indebted to Ann Pasternak Slater for help in translating Pushkin's 'To Chaadaeff'.

Under Creon

Rhododendrons growing wild below a mountain
and no long high wall or trees either;
a humped road, bone-dry, with no one—
passing one lough and then another
where water-lilies glazed, primed like traps.

A neapish hour, I searched out gaps
in that imperial shrub: a free voice sang
dissenting green, and syllables spoke
holm oaks by a salt shore, their dark tangs
glistening like Nisus in a night attack.

The daylight gods were never in this place
and I had pressed beyond my usual dusk
to find a cadence for the dead: McCracken,
Hope, the northern starlight, a death mask
and the levelled grave that Biggar traced;

like an epic arming in an olive grove
this was a stringent grief and a form of love.
Maybe one day I'll get the hang of it
and find joy, not justice, in a snapped connection,
that Jacobin oath on the black mountain.

'What Kind of Formation are B Specials?'

The franked letter
lay on the chill tiles
like a writ:
I bent to lift it and saw
this different mark—
magenta and military—
across one corner,
then split the edge and read,
Warszawa, 9/12/81.
Yards off, a train leant
on ice and metal,
and I was a zero
in a safe house
asking who was it
crossed the packed snow
with this misdirected, late,
uncandid message
to Anglia, their Anglia?
That fremd evening
I tried to connect
the signs under my eyes
with the state official
who'd scanned your lines,
for now that I've learnt
the oppressor's alphabet
I live in the half-light
of a strange
shivering translation
where the kingdom of letters

is like the postal system
of a frozen state
and your last question
slips through like code.
Now I go down
among the glubbed carp
of catholic Europe
that taste of mud and penance
this Christmas Eve,
and in the belly
of a non-nation
admire a chosen hunger . . .
but I still can't pray,
end, or send this letter.

Desertmartin

At noon, in the dead centre of a faith,
Between Draperstown and Magherafelt,
This bitter village shows the flag
In a baked absolute September light.
Here the Word has withered to a few
Parched certainties, and the charred stubble
Tightens like a black belt, a crop of Bibles.

Because this is the territory of the Law
I drive across it with a powerless knowledge—
The owl of Minerva in a hired car.
A Jock squaddy glances down the street
And grins, happy and expendable,
Like a brass cartridge. He is a useful thing,
Almost at home, and yet not quite, not quite.

It's a limed nest, this place. I see a plain
Presbyterian grace sour, then harden,
As a free strenuous spirit changes
To a servile defiance that whines and shrieks
For the bondage of the letter: it shouts
For the Big Man to lead his wee people
To a clean white prison, their scorched tomorrow.

Masculine Islam, the rule of the Just,
Egyptian sand dunes and geometry,
A theology of rifle-butts and executions:
These are the places where the spirit dies.
And now, in Desertmartin's sandy light,
I see a culture of twigs and bird-shit
Waving a gaudy flag it loves and curses.

As a White Lodge in a Garden
of Cucumbers

Voluble in a slum,
in a garlic opera
where paper roses
fall from a tarnished ceiling
and the room smells
of roasting ptarmigan,
capsicums, and songs
juicy as peaches,

these lazy painters
have slipped off
to take a sly poke
at the soft pedagogues.
It is time, they sing,
to praise the surface,
the pure and twisting
figure-of-eight that curves

the sun within itself.
They strip to irony
and clever laughter
in a comedy of oil.
Hilarious, his prong;
what a scream her fanny is;
though the senna teacher
squeaks, why aren't they serious?

Exogamy

'could be the site, this,
a scuffy sort of place
where the dialect's bloat,
raffish, or foxed at the edges;
not like the buff stoat
that's chasing something
on the other side
of the biffy road—
appetite stretched out
to the thing it is.
An orange windsock flups
over the perimeter
and grey aircadets jump
from an alum pod,
a scatter-fall
like holy water
dropping on a petrol dump.
Here there's neither priest,
nor bottled padré—
just some short steps
to a low stage
in a farty hardboard hut
where your head's been cropped
and mine's in a bandage:
fuck, let them drop us.

Descendancy

All those family histories
are like sucking a polo mint—
you're pulled right through
a tight wee sphincter
that loses you.
e.g. I've a second cousin
drives a prowl car
in downtown Vancouver,
and another's the local rozzer
in a place called Buxton.
Could be that a third one
—say an ex-B Special—
has pulled up at a roadblock
a shade far from Garrison?

The Book of Juniper

In the original liturgy
on a bare island

a voice seeks an answer
in the sea wind:

"The tides parted and I crossed
barefoot to Inishkeel.

Where was the lost crozier
among the scorched bracken?

And where was that freshet
of sweet water?

Goose-grass and broken walls
were all my sanctuary,

I mistook a drowsed hour
for the spirit's joy;

on a thymy headland
I entered

the strict soul
of a dry cricket.

Heat haze and wild flowers,
a warm chirring all

that civil afternoon,
till its classic song

failed me and I sighed
for a different love

in grey weather."

*

"Place the yeasty word
between my lips,

give me comfort
in a sheepfold,

shelter me
in a mild grove."

*

"There is no word
and no comfort.

Only a lichened stone
is given you,

and juniper,
green juniper."

*

Tougher than the wind
it keeps a low profile
on rough ground.
Rugged, fecund,
with resined spines,
the gymnosperm
hugs the hillside
and wills its own survival.
The subtle arts are still to happen
and in the eye of a needle
a singing voice
tells a miniature epic
of the boreal forest:
not a silk tapestry
of fierce folk
warring on the tundra
or making exquisite love
on a starry counterpane,
but an in-the-beginning
was a wintry light
and *juniperus*.

*

On the brown hills
above a Roman spa
in Austro-Hungaria
the savin hides
its berries of blue wax
in a thorny crown,

while in the rapt
shaded casino
a small black ball
skips and ricochets
like a sniper's bullet.

Jug-ears and jowls,
walrus moustaches, frowns—
those gravid urns
on clotted mahogany.
What mineral water can soothe
a tetchy liver or a glum colon?

The wheel flicks,
the hard pea itches;
in the gummed hotel
fingers dibble and thrust
like sappers pushing
through primed earth.

Later, the dry scrape
of an empty tumbler
locked on a ouija board
will spell out a dead yes
like chalk on a billiard cue.

The wind riffles the savin;
the humid band begins to play.

*

A clear and tearful fluid,
the bittersweet genièvre
is held to a wet window
above a college garden.

On the lazy shores
of a tideless sea,
the Phoenician juniper
burns a fragrant incense
in a sandy nest.

And in a Zen garden
all the miniature trees
have the perfect despair
of bound feet.

Exiled in Voronezh
the leavening priest of the Word
receives the Host on his tongue—
frost, stars, a dark berry,
and the sun is buried at midnight.

*

On a bruised coast
I crush a blue bead
between my fingers,
tracing the scent, somewhere,
of that warm mnemonic haybox,
burnished fields, a linen picnic
and a summer dawn
where mushrooms raise their domed gills.
They are white in the dew
and this nordic grape
whets an eager moment

of bodies meeting in a fishy fume.
Its meek astringency is distilled
into perfume and medicines,
it matches venison
as the sour gooseberry
cuts the oily mackerel.
Spicy, glaucous,
its branches fan out
like the wind's shadow
on long grass,
then melt back
and go to ground
where swart choughs
open their red beaks,
stinging the air
with stony voices.

*

Though it might be a simple
decoration
or a chill fragrance
in a snug souterrain,
I must grasp again
how its green
springy resistance
ducks its head down and skirts
the warped polities of other trees
bent in the Atlantic wind.
For no one knows
if nature allowed it
to grow tall

what proud grace
the juniper tree might show
that flared, once, like fire
along the hills.

*

On this coast
it is the only
tree of freedom
to be found,
and I imagine
that a swelling army is marching
from Memory Harbour and Killala
carrying branches
of green juniper.

Consider
the gothic zigzags
and brisk formations
that square to meet
the green tide rising
through Mayo and Antrim,

now dream
of that sweet
equal republic
where the juniper
talks to the oak,
the thistle,
the bandaged elm,
and the jolly jolly chestnut.

27

A Brackish New Year

In the bistre bistro
the cane chairs
are the colour of a bad cigar,
and all the talk
in the café europe
is of a new sweet style:
the day's newspapers
turning in a brown study
to epic form.

Each day is charred
more than the one before,
and that photographer
might be a yellow *flâneur*
on a Victorian street
where poems can speak
both the green academy
and the iceworks,
where the opera house
slips down his throat
like an aimless oyster
and, at long last,
the work might begin.

After the Summit

"Wee buns and no harm, friend,
this's a contraceptive epic
where the *Fanny* sleaks up the Elbe
for a yarn wi'the Kaiser
(it's his Mausers she's after).
The boul Jimmy, your man Craig,
keeks at his briar and maybe dreams
that he's captain of a lifeboat:
an oiled hero, but'n uniform,
and a dacent ould skin."

*

Boot polish and the Bible,
the Boys' Brigade is arming.
This is the album you found
in your grandmother's sideboard,
the deedbox with her burial papers,
a humped ledger and a lock
of that dead uncle's hair.
There is so little history
we must remember who we are.

Politik

The headmaster of a national school
chalks *Ginkel* on the blackboard
as a flag snicks a big *NO*
over the mudflats and barracks;
the city is like a locked yard
that's caked with grey pigeon-cack;
the Chief stalks, stalks, like the Kaiser
and crowds bristle at the docks.
Krekk! kkrek! the stubborn particles
trek through my carbon-dater,
each chipping past like a spiked curse
stamped with these numbers: 1–9–1–2.

I'd be dead chuffed if I could catch
the dialects of those sea-loughs,
but I'm scared of all that's hard
and completely subjective:
those quartzy voices in the playground
of a school called Rosetta Primary
whose basalt and sandstone have gone
like Napoleon into Egypt.

Argument from Design

Your glooby voice
is salt and carrageen,
a dolphin fountain
among the bay trees
in a Tuscan garden
where a dwarf on a tortoise
guards the pearly grotto;
and your quaint frizz
has this ebony wrinkle
glazed with bruised purple,
an aubergine lip,
a barbel-beard.
What a baroque smörgåsbord!
bad taste of the blond north
doing a flip
with the sugars of the deep south.

Father of History

A state schoolroom and a master talking
in a limber voice, a spiky burr
like a landrail crecking in the bracken.
Ock there he is with hair like furze,
smiling obliquely on the risen town
and building Lisburn like a warm
plain-spoken sermon on the rights of man.
A sunned Antrim face, he maybe prays
to the New Light in a relished dialect,
the eager accent of a free sept,
broken in the north, in resurrection.
Folded like bark, like cinnamon things,
I traced them to the Linen Hall stacks—
Munro, Hope, Porter and McCracken;
like sweet yams buried deep, these rebel minds
endure posterity without a monument,
their names a covered sheugh, remnants, some
                                    brackish signs.

Off the Back of a Lorry

A zippo lighter
and a quilted jacket,
two rednecks troughing
in a gleamy diner,
the flinty chipmarks
on a white enamel pail,
Paisley putting pen to paper
in Crumlin jail,
a jumbo double
fried peanut butter
sandwich Elvis scoffed
during the last
diapered days—
they're more than tacky,
these pured fictions,
and like the small ads
in a country paper
they build a gritty
sort of prod baroque
I must return to
like my own boke.

A Rum Cove, a Stout Cove

On the Barrack Islands far out
in the South Atlantic
the great-great-grandson (Sol Grout)
of Nelson's last bosun
is packing crawfish into a thick
barnacled keepbox marked *Briton
Kanning Factors Illimitated*.
It's his swart locks and cochin cheeks
that glim in the top left-hand corner
of "Bold Bessie", the prime banner
that longs to LOL 301.
Like Gib, like the god called M'Lud,
and those tars behind locked doors
whistling *Britannia Rules*
in their slow skrimshandering
with worn and corded tools,
he's firm, Sol Grout, to the core,
the genius of these used islands
where no maritime elegists sing
of Resolution or Independence
with their harbourmaster's stores,
clagged mountains of ashy shale
and a small bird that noone has named—
a flightless timorous landrail
whose cry is rusted, hard, like chains.

Black Bread

(for Ann Pasternak Slater) .

Splitting birches, spiky thicket, kinship—
this is the passionate, the phonic surface
I can take only on trust, like a character
translated to a short story whose huge language
he doesn't know. So we break black bread
in the provinces and can't be certain
what it is we're missing, or what sacrament
this might be, the loaf wrapped in a shirt-tail
like a prisoner's secret or a caked ikon,
that is sour and good, and has crossed over versts,
kilometres, miles. It's those journeys
tholed under the salt stars, in the eager wind
that starves sentries and students in their long coats.
Claudius is on the phone, hear that hard
accent scraping its boots on the threshold,
his thick acid voice in your uncle's conscience,
I'd have known better how to defend my friend.
Bitter! Bitter! Bitter! the wedding-guests chant
in bast sandals, the pickled cucumbers
cry out in a prickly opera and round grains
of coriander stud the desert crust.
It's a lump of northern peat, itself alone,
and kin to the black earth, to shaggy speech;
I'll taste it on my tongue next year in the holy,
freed city of gold and parchment.

Yes, the Maternity Unit

In a middling hour, Wednesday's raw afternoon
      of kitchen buildings and a green pitch,
my autopod smooths along a metalled slant
        between beds of tame juniper.

A geometry of poplars sifts in the wind,
      their tight theorem almost surprised
as it fences ten flat playing-fields
        on the sour edge of town.

The thin trunks level out in a zero air
      to a plumed stillness: corporation railings
or the fixed bayonet of a sentry
        erect at a border-post.

This is that secular republic of observations,
      its pedestrian optics a stick trilled
by a careless boy along stiff kinetic spikes
        that line a public space.

Bored by enclosures, he machines a burst of fire
      in the strumming light, sighting discipline
on the horizon, like the idea of barracks.
        By his rippling fence

I pop the question again: can this nissen plain,
      this fifties boredom by a dual carriageway,
really be a poetic? Must every civic
        eye unpeel

36

identical versions of the same damned spot?
      How can a row of poplars on a green field,
   limed rectangles and a railway line
       stretched tight across

a listless hinterland scutched with canals
      —how can this straight-and-narrow ground be changed
by some brisk buffer with a skill? Tell me this,
      yes tell me this.

*

limp king dick has got the chop
but Quim and Bum must slog it out
like two bloodied armies—
oh that intimate close combat
of knees blades and buggering spikes!
as, straining in its slimy burrow,
a knotted fisty-face punches
out of their racking scrum:
wet-thatched, a spiky tuft,
a red red urchin,
its first cry is the cry
of a drenched starling
that splinters, crack-splinters like a light-switch!

*

37

Behind sealed windows
each tiny grub must yell
inside a plastic cell,
be topped and tailed
before its feed
and with a goldfish mouth
gnaw the embossed nipple
on a tender shield,
until, heavy-headed,
a clubbed frown,
it contemplates the wind
and blurps a verdict.

Then a milky sleep will come
—pure, unembellished,
a cotton being
within the domed baroque
of azure gilt and swirling putti,
a tide of tufty-tails and yellow motions
that smell of warm fudge.

It breaks and changes
to a beetroot scream with flipper limbs,
a ringing tone
that pumps the suburb to a strange balloon.

*

Villas and boxed gardens,
lawns, stretched canvas,
a civic grid of plane trees,
then boredom, grey flannel
and the terror of light verse,
till it happens as the Sabbath dream
of that most gentle and retired
customs official who brushed aside
the brass buttons on his blue dolman.
Now the wires sag between their thickened poles
and a zinc tune hums
in mugs of veined porcelain,
as a brown train chunters
past a tulip farm
where buds wax
to a drift of sperm
before each bloom
turns to the feeding sun
and gapes like a scaldy—

speak, speak, wee yahweh,
from out your sleepy Egypt.

A Written Answer

This poem by Rupert Brookeborough
is all about fishing and the stout B-men
(they live for always in our hearts,
their only crime was being loyal),
there is a lough in it and stacks of rivers,
also a brave wee hymn to the sten-gun.
The poet describes Gough of the Curragh
and by his use of many metric arts
he designs a fictionary universe
which has its own laws and isn't quite
the same as this place that we call real.
His use of metonymy is pretty desperate
and the green symbolism's a contradiction,
but I like his image of the elm and chestnut,
for to me this author is a fly man
and the critics yonder say his work is alright.

Cinnamon Stick

Like a ghost in a gaberdine
the mnemonist comes hunching
over the smooth grass: oh, he breathes,
I hear psalms in the suburbs;
behold those virgin players
in a drift of light. Lazy
butterflies, they are, white flipflops
dancing on the bouncy green;
their blancoed grace, it bobs and spins
in a pure balsa playing. How
this flutters above the haycocks.
I am a chalk man, but; I rise
smoothly from my tomb of vellum,
its sigil a lavender sprig
on a pumice glans: my dreams
web through private libraries
of ancient erotica, pungent
as dolphins anchored on a wave
of bay leaves. I am the nephew
of another nephew, and my
tobacco rhetoric must creak
a dusty music from my lust.
Only Christ, the spirit of the forms,
shivers the surface like a shoal
of fry. He will not answer me;
and I must lay this body down
like a brown whiskered nightjar
shadowing bark and perished leaves.

Manichean Geography I

Consider a coral or guano atoll
Where a breezy Union Jack
Flaps above the police station.

There is a rusting mission hut
Built out of flattened tin cans
(Bully beef, beans and tomato pilchards)

Where the Reverend Bungo Buller
And his prophet, Joe Gimlet,
Preach the gospel of cargoes.

They worship a white god
Of dentures and worn toothbrushes
Who will come to earth, Hallelulia,

In a reconditioned Flying Fortress
Humping bales of fresh calico
And a crate of Black and Deckers.

Seeding like brisk parachutes,
The ancestral spirits will fall
From the pod of an airship,

And the chosen people will serve
Themselves with orange jube-jubes
In a brand-new discount warehouse.

Manichean Geography II

Banal hours in muggy weather.
The slack wind—warm, trammelled—
Is named for a freighter
That dumped its clotted chains
In Prince Darling Bay.
One time, sometime, never again old chug.

From a rainwood pulpit
The Reverend Spanner McTavish
Preaches a burnt sermon
On the injustice of the Copra Board
While an Anglican head-hunter
Reads *Phrenology Made Easy*
And fidgets with his namba.
One time, sometime, never again old chug.

Sunset and a frigate-bird
Circling the chalk lighthouse.
In a twilight of flying foxes
The coconut crabs are shredding
O-level papers in English Literature,
As a pidgin ode is chanted
In the deepy rainforest
To a signed photograph
Of his High Troppo Majesty
The Duke of Edinburgh.
One time, sometime, never again old chug.

To bossy saltmen from wayback
The islands are a spatched necklace
Of prickly heat, boils,
And choggy boredom.
Big Ben Man, where is?
Asks the girl whose white teeth
Have the blank snowy dazzle
Of coconut flesh.
Just look what we've made
Of your damned islands, we answer.
They are images now
—Never again old chug—
Images of our own disgust.

A Nation, Yet Again

(after Pushkin)

That kitsch lumber-room is stacked
with a parnassian dialect:
"love, hope, and quiet reputation
kissed us for a short season
and the gamey letters that we swopped,
in clipped verse, soon had to stop."
No one, then, praised either side,
though some dipped down among the shades
to find Aeneas and to file
a delicate, a tough, new style
that draws the language to the light
and purifies its tribal rites.
I'm tense now: talk of sharing power,
prophecies of civil war,
new reasons for a secular
mode of voicing the word *nation*
set us on edge, this generation,
and force the poet to play traitor
or act the half-sure legislator.
No matter; there's a classic form
that's in the blood, that makes me warm
to better, raise, build up, refine
whatever gabbles without discipline:
see, it takes me now, these hands stir
to bind the northern to the southern stars.

L'Envie de Commencement

Dactyls and the light of harbours:
how simple it is in the beginning
for the historian to walk at dawn,
seeing a pure narrative before him.

Local Histories

A khaki bell-tent in the mopane forest:
Professor "Deeko" Kerr is on vacation
Observing the delicate birds of Africa.
He leaves his russet hide to take a leak,
"What I have, I hold," he thinks as the boy
Sneaks a quick gander at his pinko prong.
Chit-chat evaporates at this charred altitude
Like letters airmailed to Great Namaland
Or Deeko's postcards to his old headmaster
Who wrote the school would be most pleased to learn
Of his promotion to the Chair of Social Justice
At Jan Smuts College in the Orange Free State.
He thanked him also for his learned article,
"Samuel Twaddell: a Co. Down Man at the Cape".
Even now, at a bring-and-buy in Cleaver Park,
His Aunt Mina is telling Lady Lowry,
"That boy's gone far, but we've heard nothing yet."

A Daily Beauty

*Before he emigrated to Philadelphia, John Dunlap, the printer of
the Declaration of Independence, was an apprentice in Gray's
printing-shop in Main Street.*

A tray of waspy plums and American apples,
three yards of cracked oilcloth tacked to the counter,
that mild pong of ham, pan loaves, the paraffin tang
of newsprint from a stack of sisalled papers:
the *Derry Journal*, *Weekly News*, and *Strabane Chronicle*.
It's buzzy slapdash in and out: a private's squatting
on an elsan in the sangar by the humpy bridge,
as *Bannigan's Gravels* rakes through its gear-box
and the auctioneer's voice drills the clabbery market
like a scorching lark over a prison yard.
There's Union Street and Barrack Street, and here's me
just an ignoramus with a jammy piece,
taking a holyer in these slurried townlands.

Presbyterian Study

A lantern-ceiling and quiet.
I climb here often and stare
At the scoured desk by the window,
The journal open
At a date and conscience.

It is a room without song
That believes in flint, salt,
And new bread rising
Like a people who share
A dream of grace and reason.

A bit starchy perhaps.
A shade chill, like a draper's shop.
But choosing the free way,
Not the formal,
And warming the walls with its knowing.

Memory is a moist seed
And a praise here, for they live,
Those linen saints, lithe radicals,
In the bottled light
Of this limewashed shrine.

Hardly a schoolroom remembers
Their obstinate rebellion;
Provincial historians
Scratch circles on the sand,
And still, with dingy smiles,

We wait on nature,
Our jackets a dungy pattern
Of mud and snapped leaves,
Our state a jacked corpse
Committed to the deep.

Of Difference Does it Make

*During the 51-year existence of the Northern Ireland Parliament
only one Bill sponsored by a non-Unionist member was ever
passed.*

Among the plovers and the stonechats
protected by the Wild Birds Act
of nineteen-hundred-and-thirty-one,
there is a rare stint called the notawhit
that has a schisty flight-call, like the chough's.
Notawhit, notawhit, notawhit
—it raps out a sharp code-sign
like a mild and patient prisoner
pecking through granite with a teaspoon.

For the Kilogram of the Archives

Maybe the south of this city
is like the French Quarter in Oran
and longs to cross the water
or believes it's already there.
   On a hot-hot afternoon
when the sky is a cyanic punishment
for the harmless sins of Onan
it boggles in a warp of air:
watchtowers, a starched building, date-palms
and the doodled script of railings
over a cartesian square.
   That figure in the white burnous
and smoked glasses, is the shady historian
who is known as Dr Noone
(all his works have been translated
from the original Volapuk).
He is able to recite the Koran
backwards in a high-pitched voice
and in the era of bad intentions
he was tried for failed sodomy.
   On the penultimate page
of *Plato and Exact History*
he argues that the absolute
is like a rod of pure platinum:
This monogod is a rational being,
more of a nogod than a sacred dingdong;
it is likely that He hears our psalms,
though His Justice is not perfect.

He writes in a walled garden
and sips Vichy water before dark.
His subject, he believes, is autarkic
and the present state is numbered
among his choice and forbidden loves.

Martello

(for Roy and Aisling Foster)

Cack-handed, like a stocious mason,
Napper Tandy picks at this coast.
A brave chiseller, that one,
he might be Nestor as *général*
in the army of the revolution.
When they captured Rutland Island
he supped poteen with the postmaster
and rapped out a proclamation
dated the first year of liberty.
His own officers laid hands on him,
rolling him back on board the *Anacréon*,
merry and bulky, like a Greek.
The same month, another calendar,
I tracked him to a stone harbour
where he slips through the salmon nets
and swims out, like a patched seal
beyond Roaninish. A boaster,
a daft eejit, but a hard taproot
that can't be shifted, he nips back
with a springy juvenescence,
his lips stained with wine, his chest wrapped
in a new, freshly dyed tricolour.

*

In an hour of difficulty
Barney McLoone rowed a German spy
across the Gweebarra;
so a line may stretch,
in that illusion of causes,
from the salmon quay at Lettermacaward
to the *oifig an phoist*
on Rutland Island.
He drew an IRA pension,
got full every night,
and took a pick to the living rock
below a breezeblock shell
thrown up by a visitor from Clogher.

*

There is a dead vigilance along this coast,
a presence that bruises like the word *British*.
You can catch the atmosphere of neglected garrisons,
and the rusted aftertaste of bully beef
in the dashed surprise of a cement watchtower
ruined on a slope of ragweed and bullocks grazing.
In the dovegrey Victorian hotel
a spooly sways at the bar and says,
"We're nearly a nation now, before the year's out
they'll maybe write Emmet's epitaph."

Can you *describe* history I'd like to know?
Isn't it a fiction that pretends to be fact
like *A Journal of the Plague Year*?
And the answer that snaps back at me
is a winter's afternoon in Dungannon,
the gothic barracks where the policemen
were signing out their weapons in a stained register,

a thick turbid light and that brisk smell of fear
as I described the accident and felt guilty—
guilty for no reason, or cause, I could think of.

*

Shaggy sandstone and wet granite,
the usualness of rhododendrons,
gravel, and liverish glumped laurels:
it's a bad day at Stormont Castle
where a twitchy civil servant
is writing to a friend in Kew.
"This might be Sir Walter Scotland—
or even very bad Tennyson—
it's being stuck in a fraud barony
only escapists would want to enter.
Bloody awful it is (or as we code it
PRETTY MAUDLING DON'T YOU THINK?).
Their accents sound like dustbins
being dragged over concrete,
though to hear them one'd think
that instead of being lumbered
with a rotten shower of prize idiots
this was God's own acre we're holding—
can you imagine? Stony bonkers, they are.
They're always saying *sorry* and *like*,
as in, *Could you please tell me, like?*
There's a rum history to blame
and it's like this the whole time—
fucking terrible in fact . . . ."

The gravel ralls; his nib's on the buzzer.
. . . must hatch a snifter: Ciao now, old cock.

*

Consider a city of disappointed bridges
and a crowd at New Year
clodding bottles at the Albert Clock
(what is it that they want to stop?)
There you are taking a slow dander
down Donegall Street:
you might be going to file your copy
or cast a vote that if he knew
your editor would call disloyal.
Most likely it's a jar you're after
and peace from all the linseed captains
do to provoke your secret laughter.

*

Action is solid: this one day in March
a hijacked saloon smacks a dozen rounds
                    into the Bunch of Grapes
                    and in Desertmartin
men in lockram masks and dark glasses
dig down through sandy soil to a bristling dump
of lumpy kapok, cortex fuse and green jerricans
                    as a meshed landrover at Clady
mounts the ramp on the humped bridge into the
                    blinding square
while the chief sub hears the pips spitting in his ear
and the real Captain Black issues a statement
                    as a corporal draws a vector
                    between Scrabo and Helen's Tower
and the dunchered skip of the *Clyde Valley* slips a short
to an invisible quartermaster in the Klondike
                    and a van waits, waits at the corner
                    of Atlantic and Baltic Avenues

all to no purpose, yet affecting a cause
                    like a stubbed toe, a cracked axle
                    or a backfiring old banger
                    for these acts must come back
                    as syntax, as grammar
                    and a temporal fiction.

*

Like lead dropping in a shot-tower
Clio's voice has no feeling,
for it isn't music, this estranged mixture
of hindsight and becoming
where crowds mass in a spent future
wearing unionjack raincoats and raising
red-white-and-blue umbrellas.
Lymphatic and nettly, like jellyfish
crowding in a duskiss tide,
their images slop against the eyes;
and what dory monsters glup to the surface,
each like a plated turd with a pilot-light.
See Brookeborough in tinted glasses
like an oily magnate, and the long fellah,
de Valera, gliding in a black car
to express regret at the death of Hitler.

From the Death Cell: Iambes VIII

(after Chénier)

We live:—dishonoured, in the shit. So what? it had to be.
    This is the pits and yet we feed and sleep.
Even here—penned in, watered and waiting for the chop
    (just place your bets)—affairs take off,
there's gossip, bitching and a pecking-order.
    Songs, jokes, card-schools; she lifts her skirts; someone
bops a tight balloon against the window-panes.
    It's like the speeches of those seven hundred eejits
(Barrère's the shiftiest of the lot)—a comic fart
    we whoop and cheer and then forget.
One jumps, another skips; that greasy pack
    of gut and gullet politicians raps and hoots
until, dead quick, the door scrakes open
    and our tiger-masters' wee pimp struts in.
Who's getting it today? We freeze and listen,
    then all but one of us knows it isn't him . . . .

The House by the Greyhound Track

(for Bernard and Heather O'Donoghue)

Love and gossip
from a wedged county:
we're taking the waters
on Naran strand,
going out on the sea
with our French *copains*
and wishing the wise old woman
would get it right.
When I post my screed
to a private placename
(the shining melt
of slipped hounds
stretched like a tapeworm
under Dev's rule),
I'll recall the tilt
of a road through a wet valley
called Béal na mBláth
and the rock at the turn
where the One
dropped a snaky pair
of rimless glasses
and a chill smile.
The wind eels
over the needlegrass
and Michael Devine
climbs to a starved zero
that is perfect
and without pity
like a prose-style

60

in the desert.
Plastic sacks and black flags
are flying over Ardara,
and would someone please tell me
if this wan bitterness
is just a fleck of angst
or the self-disgust
of the fellow-traveller?
Like his, my sleakit eyes
scan the dunes at Ballykinlar
where a tired sentry
is counting the hours
in the bored smell of marram
as he waits for the word
to strike up a bogey tune
and quickmarch, toodle-oo,
towards the breakers.

Foot Patrol, Fermanagh

A pierrepoint stretch, mid-afternoon;
the last two go facing back
down the walled street below the chestnuts
this still claggy Sabbath.
They hold their rifles lightly, like dipped rods,
and in a blurt of sunshine
the aluminium paint on the customs shed
has a dead shine like a text
brushed onto basalt.
It's not that anything will happen next
in this hour that is as constant
as sin, and as original,
though why is it they remind me
of a prisoner led singing down a corridor
to a floor that isn't a floor any longer?

At Maas

Made a shade tamer
by the sun and salt hay,
the ironstone causeway
seeps a blood-rust
this weather.
Put your ear to the ground
and you'll catch the *chthon-chthon*
that spells *must*,
a vinous sound
with a classic shape to it.
On this sandy spit
even the lugworms
are spoken for,
and the Adam form
through the trees
says, "Take up your pen,
make a new barm
and try the whole thing again.
No more talk about stock
or the joining sea,
just plant your big foot, love,
hard down on the bedrock
and give a last shove."

Signing the Treaty

A haircrack in bone china
or an eider duck's olive egg
clecking in the squeezed light:
there's a wet mildness now
like that turned earth
or the juices between your legs.

Amphion

Flame on the salt marsh,
thin chimney
like a pen, or a pencil,
it makes the surface
a planished thing
and burns, tribeless now,
over the slobland.

On a concrete apron
by the slack perimeter,
there is a line of surplus trucks,
nine gross of jerricans
under a pegged tarpaulin,
and a stack of exhaust pipes
wrapped in waxed paper.
A short man in an overcoat—
the new government auctioneer—
waddles, stops, and waddles on
like a dumpy general.

Over the road
on reclaimed space
and dry dumped earth,
there is that pointed,
unpainted sense
of real absence
that bites like a beginning.
Ah, we say, this is culture—
the flame, the hardware

and a voice
that imagines what it describes
and draws from the earth and the air
this new-strung form
that betters what we are.

And Where Do You Stand on the National Question?

"Told him the shortest way to Tara was via Holyhead."
(Stephen Dedalus)

Apple-blossom, a great spread of it
above our heads.
This blue morning a new visitor
is laidback on a deckchair;
he's civil and clever,
a flinty mandarin
being entertained, like an oxymoron,
in this walled garden.
Ecco two glasses of young wine
. . . *et on mange des asperges.*
I imagine him
as the state's intelligence,
a lean man in a linen suit
who has come to question me
for picking up a pen
and taking myself a shade seriously.
"Paisley's plain tongue, his cult
of Bunyan and blood
in blind dumps like Doagh and Boardmills—
that's the enemy."
I've an answer ready in the sun
but my eye tines the grass
for a tiny mound of soil:
the mole works underground,
a blind glove
that gropes the earth and cannot love.

67

"Your Lagan Jacobins, they've gone
with *The Northern Star*. I've heard
Hewitt and Heaney trace us back
to the Antrim weavers—
I can't come from *that*."
"Why not, though? Isn't there
this local stir in us all?—
flick of the thumb, a word's relish,
the clitoral tick of an accent,
wee lick of spit or lovejuice?
I'd call that a brave kindness."
Then a journey blows back at me—
rust-orange and green,
the Enterprise scudding north
past the brown burn of whin and bracken
till it halts and waits for clearance
under the gourly vigilance
of a corrie in bandit country—
"That's where the god, Autochthon,
is crossed by the hangman's rope."
He counters with a short fiction
called *Molyneaux's Last Hope*.
"These islands are stepping-stones
to a metropolitan home,
an archipelago that's strung
between America and Europe."
"So you're a band of Orange dandies?
Oscar in Père-Lachaise with a sash on?"
"Well, not exactly . . . that's unfair—
like my saying it's a green mess you're after."
"I want a form that's classic and secular,
the risen *République*,
a new song for a new constitution—
wouldn't you rather have that
than stay loose, baggy and British?

You don't *have* to fall back
on Burke and the Cruiser,
on a batty style
and slack o'whoozy emotion."
We hit a pause like a ramp,
shrug and mark time
before we guess the design
of life after Prior:
the last civil servant
is dropping over from Whitehall.
Call him Sir Peregrine Falkland;
he's a bit thick—not a high-flyer—
but he'll do the trick.

S/He

There's burnt ground
and a cindertrack
all along the ridge
between the shops
and the railway bridge,
like it's occupied territory
with no one around
this cold snap.
Here's a wet sheugh
smells like a used sheath,
and here's frogspawn
and a car battery
under a screggy hawthorn.
They're having a geg
chucking *weebits* and *yuk*
and laughing at the blups—
kids turned fierce
on a tip,
little hard men in boiler suits
locked in a wargame.

Yesterday I stared
at this girl with cropped hair—
a grandpa shirt on her
and lovebites on her neck,
little pinky bruises
like a rope had snagged there.

Ah shite, the bitter joy
as the plunged head gets born!—
a March wind
hits the main street
of a village called Convoy
and I'm starved
by the first screech that's torn
from out the guts of the blind poet.

*

Something in the air,
too-quiet-altogether
on the back road that slips
down into Derry.
Where that open pasture
slopes from a close wood
to a file of chestnuts
there's a counterfeit sense
that unsettles me just now.
It might be the landlord's absence
from a version of pastoral,
or the hidden scanner
that has to be somewhere.

Over the ramp
the light that bangs back
from the fieldgrey screens
has a preserved feel to it,
like radio silence
or the site of an accident.

I wind down the window,
pass proof of myself
and match
the copper stubble on his chin
with the light green
of his shirt—
may God forgive me
this parched gift of sight.

*

This hereness is to loiter
by a quay in Derry
and gaze at the spread river,
the pigeons and the pigeon-cowlings
on a stained flour mill,
until a voice whispers
in the balmy sigh of a lover,
"who's in the wrong county
like the maiden city?"

*

"Would you give us a lift, love?
it's that late n'scary . . . ."
I was only half there
like a girl after a dance,
wary, on the road to Muff.
We might've been out after curfew
in the buzzy *deux-chevaux*,
slipping past the chestnuts
on a street in provincial France.

It stuck close to me, though,
how all through the last half
a helicopter held itself
above the Guildhall—
Vershinin's lines were slewed
by the blind chopping blades,
though Olga looked chuffed
when she sighed, "Won't it be odd
with no soldiers on the streets?"

Trine

I am a rod
that won't melt,
the strict voice
of a schoolman
tensed in the pelt
of blinding song
peeled high
over a hazel grove.
My virgin logic
was never born
or made, like love;
shiny naked,
I can't be worn
down or out,
however long
the weather tries
my juicy sting:
like perfect pitch
I cannot move.
I am the light
of March skies
on a drawn bead
of mercury,
a pen digging
into steeled ground,
catgut's bite
beyond space, time,
or that empire
the heavy stranger

must call experience.
My othered argument
is a snail's jism
crossing the floor
of a clagged cell
where the patterned god
pulls tight
till I am seised
by this body's starved
brittle eyes.

Ceremony

I see the women come walking
From the town of the white river-meadow.
Their eyes are a silk fragrance;
Their ritual must appease
The squat god, Terminus.

One is shy and delicate
As she carries a bowl of wine;
And another, in the spirit's beauty,
Will transfigure the hard god
With honey on a green leaf.

He hunches at the stone bridge,
A crude surplus taskman
In a blocked sangar. His raw
Fur is grey and hackled,
His broody vigilance

The shadow of all judgement.
Rain and lichens
Have weathered him, and now
He squats like an institution—
Useful, half-wise, no longer young.

Honeyed wine and spicy cakes,
A fluid light and a fine
Twist of air—a song is rising
To a gold-bellied sail
That takes, takes and quickens us.

To the Linen Hall

After extremity
art turns social
and it's more than fashion
to voice the word *we*.
The epic yawp
hangs like an echo
of the big bang,
though now we tell children
to shun that original—
primal light, soaked green,
the slob mud
and a salt tang.
There is a ban
on philosophies of blood,
a terse demand
for arts and skills
to be understood,
and a common flow
into the new academy
which rules with a chill,
strenuous and insistent,
enforced formality.
Here we have a form
and a control
that is our own,
and on the stone steps
of that eighteenth-century,
reasoned library
we catch the classic spore

of Gibbon and new *ceps*,
the busts and statues
that might be stored
under the squares.
Our shaping brightness
is a style and discipline
that finds its tongue
in the woody desk-dawns
of fretting scholars
who pray, invisibly,
to taste the true vine
and hum gently
in holy sweetness.